Wild Anim

ORANGUTANS

NICKI CLAUSEN-GRACE

BLACK
RABBIT
BOOKS

Bolt is published by Black Rabbit Books
P.O. Box 3263, Mankato, Minnesota, 56002.
www.blackrabbitbooks.com
Copyright © 2019 Black Rabbit Books

Jennifer Besel, editor; Catherine Cates, interior
designer; Grant Gould, cover designer;
Omay Ayres, photo researcher

Library of Congress Cataloging-in-Publication Data
Names: Clausen-Grace, Nicki, author.
Title: Orangutans / by Nicki Clausen-Grace.
Description: Mankato, Minnesota : Black Rabbit Books, [2019] | Series:
Bolt. Wild animal kingdom | Audience: Ages 8-12. | Audience: Grades 4-6.
|Includes bibliographical references and index.
Identifiers: LCCN 2017032161 (print) | LCCN 2017043461 (ebook) | ISBN
9781680725582 (ebook) | ISBN 9781680724424 (library binding) | ISBN
9781680727364 (paperback)
Subjects: LCSH: Orangutans—Juvenile literature.
Classification: LCC QL737.P94 (ebook) | LCC QL737.P94 C53 2019 (print)
| DDC 599.88/3—dc23
LC record available at https://lccn.loc.gov/2017032161

Printed in China. 3/18

Image Credits
Dreamstime: Kantapat, 20;
Robhainer, Cover; iStock: GlobalP,
24 (leopard); USO, 3; Science Source:
Cyril Ruoso, 4–5; Shutterstock: airdone, 27;
Alexander Mazurkevich, 28-29; apple2499, 24
(tiger); David Evison, 19; Eric Isselee, 24 (insects), 31; GUDKOV ANDREY, 8–9, 11 (t), 23, 29,
32; jeep2499, 6 (both); Manekina Serafima, 16-17
(bkgd); Michael Shake, 13 (t); Oleg Mileev, 13 (b);
Ortis, 24 (leaves); RUKSUTAKARN studio, 24 (fruit);
Sergey Uryadnikov, 1, 24 (orangutan); tristan tan, 11
(b); vitstudio, 28 (tr); Superstock: NHPA, 12; Suzi
Eszterhas / Minden Pictures, 14
Every effort has been made to contact copyright
holders for material reproduced in this
book. Any omissions will be rectified in
subsequent printings if notice is
given to the publisher.

Contents

CHAPTER 1

A Day in the Life

High up in a tree, a big, orange animal swings in the branches. It's an orangutan. It uses its long, strong arms to move through the trees. Soon, heavy rain begins to fall. The orangutan finds a large leaf. It uses the leaf as an umbrella. When the rain is done, it goes back to swinging.

◄· · · ·How Big Is an Orangutan?

HEIGHT
ABOUT
4.5
FEET
(1 meter)

Long-Armed Apes

Orangutans are large apes. These animals have long arms. They also have hands and feet that grip like human hands.

These apes are smart too. They use their surroundings as tools. For example, some orangutans use leaves as napkins. Others use leaves to protect them from rain.

120 150 180
90 210
60 240
30 270
0 300
pounds **WEIGHT** pounds
73 to 250 POUNDS
(33 to 113 kilograms)

FLANGES (MALES ONLY)

ORANGE COAT

THUMBS

EYES

LONG
ARMS

9

CHAPTER 2

Food to Eat
and a Place to Live

Orangutans are **omnivores**. They eat plants and animals. Orangutans chew up leaves and bark. They munch insects. They even dip sticks in honey and lick it off.

Orangutans chew a certain kind of leaf to make a foam. They spread the foam on sore arms or legs to make them feel better.

Fruity Feast

Fruit is orangutans' favorite food. They eat figs and mangoes. And they love the durian fruit. This fruit smells really bad to people. But it tastes great to orangutans.

Using Tools

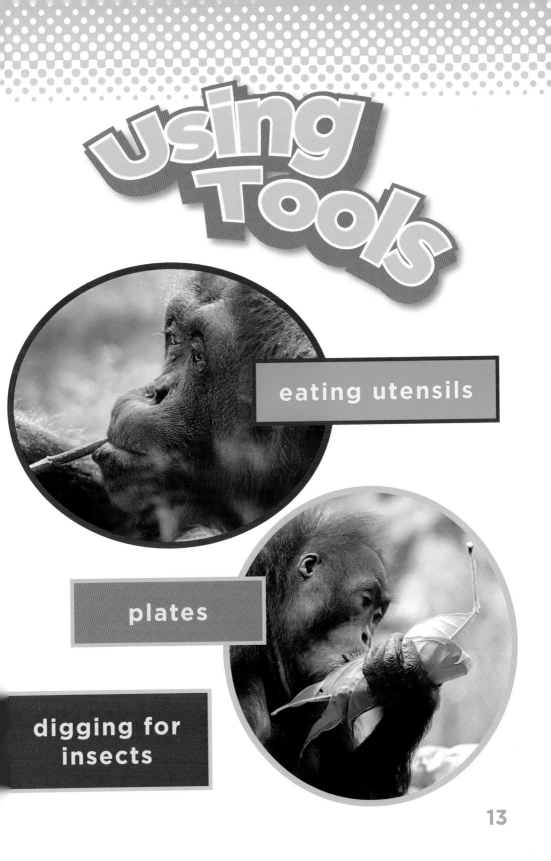

eating utensils

plates

digging for insects

Tropical Tree Houses

There are two kinds of orangutans. Bornean orangutans live in Borneo. Sumatran orangutans live in Sumatra. They live high in the rain forest trees.

Orangutans spend most of their time in the treetops. They swing from branches. Each day, they build new sleeping nests in the trees.

17

CHAPTER 3

Family Life

Orangutans usually live alone. Adult females **mate** about once every eight years. They usually have one baby at a time. Mother orangutans build strong nests for their babies. Infants cling to their mothers to get around.

COMPARING SIZES

newborn **about 3.5 POUNDS (1.6 kg)**

adult female **about 80 POUNDS (36 kg)**

pounds 0

Baby Orangutans

After about two years, young orangutans can move on their own. They **nurse** until they are up to eight years old. Just like humans, baby orangutans cry when they are hungry. They smile at their mothers too.

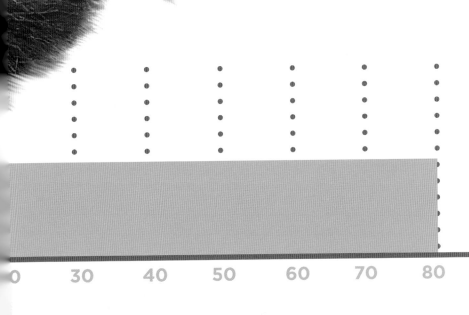

30   40   50   60   70   80

Growing Up

Young orangutans stay with their mothers for years. Their mothers have a lot to teach them. Young orangutans learn how to survive from their mothers. Females teach their young where to find food and how to build nests. Mothers also teach them which plants are safe to eat.

● ●

Young orangutans stay with their mothers until they're up to 10 years old.

Orangutan Food Chain

This food chain shows what orangutans eat. It also shows what eats orangutans.

TIGERS

LEOPARDS

ORANGUTANS

LEAVES

DURIAN FRUIT

INSECTS

CHAPTER 4

Predators
and Other Threats

Orangutans have a few wild **predators**. In Sumatra, tigers eat them. In both Sumatra and Borneo, leopards **prey** on orangutans. Tigers and leopards go after young orangutans most often.

Human Threat

People are orangutans' biggest threat. They hunt them for food and capture them for pets. People also cut down many trees. The orangutans are losing their habitats. These problems have made orangutans **endangered**.

People are taking action to save orangutans. They are making laws against hurting the apes. They are also setting aside land for orangutans to live on. Hopefully these changes can save this amazing animal.

There are fewer than 120,000 orangutans
left in the wild.

By the Numbers

NEARLY

97

PERCENT OF **DNA** ORANGUTANS SHARE WITH HUMANS

30 to 40 YEARS
LIFE SPAN IN THE WILD

4 to 5
NUMBER OF BABIES A FEMALE ORANGUTAN HAS IN ITS LIFETIME

UP TO 6 HOURS
time an orangutan spends looking for food each day

32 TEETH

DNA—acids in cells that create the traits, qualities, or features of a person or thing

endangered (in-DAYN-jurd)—close to becoming extinct

mate (MAYT)—to join together to produce young

nurse (NURS)—to drink milk from the mother's body

omnivore (AHM-ni-vor)—an animal that eats both plants and animals

predator (PRED-uh-tuhr)—an animal that eats other animals

prey (PRAY)—to catch and eat something

BOOKS

Marshall, Deb. *Orangutans.* Amazing Primates. New York: AV2 by Weigl, 2014.

Raum, Elizabeth. *Orangutans Build Tree Nests.* Animal Builders. Mankato, MN: Amicus, 2018.

Swinging Smarties. Guess What. Ann Arbor, MI: Cherry Lake Publishing, 2017.

WEBSITES

Orangutans
orangutan.org/orangutan-facts/

Orangutans
www.nationalgeographic.com/animals/mammals/group/orangutans/

Watch Orangutans Build Umbrellas, "Kiss-Squeak," and More
www.youtube.com/watch?v=3hfkDJ-r3DQ

INDEX